Authoritheocracy

in America

René Díaz-Corzo

I hold immense gratitude for everyone who showed remarkable patience and tolerance, engaging in occasionally passionate yet consistently constructive theoretical discussions. These interactions have not only highlighted shortcomings and radicalism in our government representatives but have also provided indications of potential remedies.

CONTENTS

	Acknowledgments	i
1	AUTHORITHEOCRACY	1
2	IDEOLOGICAL RIGIDITIES	15
3	POLITICAL POLARIZATION	38
4	RIGHT TO PRIVACY	60
5	WOKE	93
6	SCOTUS	127

ACKNOWLEDGMENTS

I want to extend my sincere appreciation to all individuals who have made valuable contributions to this project, whether through direct or indirect means. Of particular significance is the sense of tranquility that goes with the recognition and warm reception by loved ones who perceive the evolution within you as you engage deeply in the endeavor of translating your experiences into coherent prose.

Your unwavering support, encouragement, and astute perspectives have played a pivotal role in the realization of this endeavor. I express my gratitude for your integral involvement in this artistic odyssey.

The most pressing threat to America today is not communism, as portrayed by the right, or socialism; instead, it lies in the endeavors and actions that push America towards a fascist theocracy. This political trajectory gives rise to serious apprehensions on the erosion of democratic principles, individual freedoms, and the crucial separation of church and state.

The potential hazards of aligning a particular

religious moral code with legislation are of paramount concern in a system that values representation, inclusivity, and the protection of individual rights and liberties. Democracy thrives on the principle of pluralism, fostering an environment where diverse perspectives, beliefs, and opinions can coexist harmoniously within society. The clear rise of a fascist theocracy in states showing authoritarian tendencies presents a clear and immediate threat to democratic principles. This is due to the integration of religious beliefs with state authority, which undermines the foundations of democracy. This convergence places minority groups in jeopardy of marginalization and fosters an environment of intolerance and exclusion.

In the context of a democratic society, safeguarding the principles of democracy is of paramount importance. Democracy is a system of governance where power is vested in the hands of the people, allowing them to take part in decision-making processes and elect representatives to enact laws and policies that reflect their interests and values.

One critical aspect of preserving democracy is ensuring the separation of church and state. The concept of the separation of church and state is founded on the principle that there should be a clear distinction and independence between religious institutions and government institutions. This means that religious organizations and religious leaders should not have direct control or influence over the government, and vice versa.

It is of paramount importance to safeguard the principles of democracy as they are essential for supporting a fair and just society. Preserving the separation of church and state is an integral part of upholding religious freedom, ensuring equality for all citizens, and preventing the dominance of any belief system.

Promoting civic education holds immense importance as it equips individuals with critical thinking skills, empowering them to assess policies and political narratives beyond superficial acceptance or rejection. It encourages people to actively question, evaluate, and challenge assumptions, beliefs, and arguments, leading to logical and dependable conclusions that align with democratic principles. Furthermore, safeguarding an independent judiciary plays a pivotal role in supporting a system of checks and balances to prevent potential abuses of power. An unbiased and autonomous judiciary ensures that legislative actions are in harmony with the constitution and uphold individual rights. In combination, these two components form the bedrock of a thriving democratic society. Civic education empowers citizens to take part actively in shaping their governance and policies, while an independent judiciary ensures that the rule of law prevails, safeguarding the rights and freedoms of individuals.

However, in several states of the union, the rhetoric and legislation on this matter have significantly gained momentum and transformed into a considerable fanatical political movement. Regardless of how someone perceives their actions and agenda accomplishments as relatively insignificant in shaping our society's overall livelihood, it is essential to acknowledge that they are indeed making a discernible impact with selective effects in certain aspects of our society. This impact should not be overlooked or underestimated.

Currently, the United States' democracy and its democratic system are upheld by various political and institutional structures that support democratic principles. These structures include laws, the constitution, political parties, electoral processes, and mechanisms easing citizen participation in governance. However, the nation faces a significant challenge as some public figures employ political oratory to provoke opposition and gauge public support for a risky endeavor: a hybrid of authoritarianism and theocracy called

"Authoritheocracy." This socio-political experiment looks to blend elements of authoritarian rule and theocratic principles, posing a serious threat to the country's democratic foundations.

The hypothetical term of Authoritheocracy is important for the sake of this dissertation, it is crucial to thoroughly examine and analyze the impact of the combination even if it may initially seem relatively insignificant. This proposed term implies a system of government where a single authoritative figure or small group holds absolute power and combines it with religious or divine authority, ruling the state based on religious principles or divine guidance. It would suggest a regime that enforces strict control over both political and religious aspects of society. In a Authoritheocratic system, the governance of the state would be shaped by religious doctrines or institutions, resulting in a distinctive amalgamation of authoritarian rule and theocratic principles. It is important to emphasize that this term is purely fictional and not an existing form of government. Nevertheless, it serves as a conceptual representation of a hypothetical regime, which might not currently exist, but could be relevant in the context of ongoing movements with radical agendas that endorse, advocate for, and look to implement such a philosophy. They do so by engaging in divisive rhetoric and taking actions that undermine the checks and balances set up by democratic structures.

The convergence of a religious moral code with right-wing extremism worsens the threat to democracy. The essence of right-wing extremism often entails an authoritarian approach, emphasizing hierarchical structures, and prioritizing the interests of a select few over the broader populace. Such a concentration of power goes against the principles of democratic governance, where power is derived from and held by the people.

In a democratic society, the separation of

church and state is vital to preserving religious freedom and preventing the dominance of any belief system. By upholding this separation, the government ensures that no religious group gains a monopoly on political power, and laws are enacted based on reason, evidence, and the common good rather than dogma and religious ideology.

The danger of moving towards autocratheocracy lies in the possibility of curtailing civil liberties and human rights. For instance, policies influenced by an extreme right-wing religious ideology may infringe upon reproductive rights, LGBTQ+ rights, and the rights of marginalized communities. This creates an environment that stifles freedom of expression and undermines the democratic principle of inclusivity.

From a democratic perspective, the key to countering the threat of autocratheocracy lies in active citizen engagement and robust defense of democratic institutions. In defending democracy against the rise of autocratheocracy, it is crucial to support a strong and independent judiciary. The judiciary serves as a check on the potential abuse of power, ensuring that legislation aligns with the constitution and respects individual rights.

To translate rhetoric into action, we must take tangible measures to tackle the pressing concerns at hand. In recent years, the Republican party has shown a troubling inclination towards embracing autocracy and extremism, making it even more imperative to act decisively. Unfortunately, there seems to be little sign of this trend moderating in the foreseeable future. An example of this is clear in Florida, where books have been removed from school shelves, reflecting a manifestation of extremism, a desire for authoritarian leadership, and a prevalence of antidemocratic beliefs in the country. The parallels between the Republican Party and various autocratheocracy movements that have appeared across the nation are not hard to find, as they share certain similarities for diverse reasons.

To counter the growth of autocratheocracy in the United States, a comprehensive examination of the following measures is imperative:

1. A complete overhaul of the Electoral College, as its current structure allows sparsely populated states to exert disproportionate influence, enabling the Republican party to wield significant power without securing national majorities.

2. A thorough reformation of the process for appointing justices to the Supreme Court, ensuring greater transparency and safeguarding against potential partisan manipulation.

Addressing these issues is crucial in safeguarding democratic principles and fostering a more representative and fair political system in the country.

A political organization that perpetuates an "us-versus-them" outlook, positioning itself as the sole valid catalyst for societal transformation and advancement, is bound to cultivate a profound sense of collective identity and cohesion among its members, while simultaneously estranging dissenting voices. As time passes, the party's ideological foundations tend to grow increasingly rigid and dogmatic, leaving minimal space for dissent or alternative perspectives. Deviating from the party's prescribed beliefs and conforming to the leader's directives becomes an unyielding expectation, with any form of deviation being met with reproach or punitive measures.

By fostering an exclusivist narrative, the political party seeks to forge a strong internal bond among its followers, appealing to a shared sense of purpose and common objectives. This cohesion can, in turn, generate a powerful sense of unity and belonging within the party's ranks, bolstering their determination and dedication to the organization's mission.

However, this divisive approach inevitably leads

to the alienation of dissenting voices and marginalized perspectives. Individuals who express differing ideas or constructive criticism may find themselves ostracized or silenced, hindering the party's potential for open dialogue and growth through diverse viewpoints.

As the party's ideology hardens, critical thinking and nuanced discussions become scarce, stifling innovation and progress. The lack of receptiveness to new ideas and alternative approaches can ultimately impede the party's ability to adapt to evolving challenges or respond to the changing needs of the electorate.

A political party that nurtures an "us-versus-them" mentality may initially foster identity and unity within its ranks, but it risks compromising the values of pluralism and open discourse. The potential consequences encompass increased polarization, limited adaptability, and an erosion of democratic principles in favor of unwavering loyalty to the party's leadership and doctrines.

In the realm of political parties, ideological rigidity signifies an unwavering adherence to a specific set of beliefs or principles, devoid of space for meaningful discourse, debate, or evolution. When a party succumbs to prominent levels of ideological rigidity, it creates an atmosphere where dissenting voices are marginalized or suppressed, and alternative viewpoints are summarily dismissed. This rigid stance can be effectively exploited by a charismatic leader who proclaims their own beliefs as the sole valid and correct ones, effectively discouraging critical thinking and independent judgment among party members.

Such a leader often tries to combine their power and keep control by enforcing stringent conformity to the party's ideology. They bolster loyalty among members and foster a sense of exclusivity or exceptionalism, asserting that the party has an inherent superiority over others. This strategy aims to forge a tightly knit group that adheres unquestioningly to the leader's vision and discourages any deviation from the prescribed beliefs.

The consequences of ideological rigidity and the influence of a charismatic leader can be far-reaching. A lack of open dialogue and intellectual flexibility hampers the party's ability to adapt to changing circumstances or consider alternative perspectives. By stifling diverse viewpoints and critical thinking, the leader perpetuates an environment of conformity, which impedes the party's ability for growth and innovation.

Ideological rigidity alone may not be the first trigger for the transformation of an entire political party into a cult, but it is a noteworthy factor that significantly contributes to the emergence of cult-like characteristics within members of the party. The specific sequence of steps leading to this transformation can vary, but it is often seen that ideological rigidity takes root due to the influence exerted by the cult leader and the dynamics that develop among the group.

When a political party becomes highly rigid in its adherence to a particular ideology, it creates an environment where dissenting voices are marginalized, alternative perspectives are dismissed, and critical discussions are stifled. This rigidity sets up a fertile ground for the emergence of cult-like tendencies. The cult leader capitalizes on this ideological inflexibility to solidify their influence and control over party members.

The cult leader employs various tactics to bolster their authority and enforce conformity within the party. They present their own beliefs as absolute truths, leaving no room for questioning or debate. By discouraging critical thinking and independent judgment, the cult leader ensures a compliant and loyal following. They instill a sense of exclusivity and exceptionalism within the party, convincing members that they own unique insights and solutions.

The interplay of the cult leader's influence and the group dynamics further strengthens the grip of ideological rigidity. The leader fosters an environment where dissent is suppressed, conformity is rewarded, and a shared enemy or "us-versus-them" mentality is cultivated. This creates a sense of unity and identity within the party, while isolating members from outside perspectives and critical evaluation.

While ideological rigidity may not be the sole determinant, its presence significantly contributes to the development of a political party showing cult-like characteristics. It sets up the foundation upon which the cult leader builds their influence, manipulates group dynamics, and molds the party into a closed and dogmatic entity.

Throughout history, charismatic leaders and their inner circles have employed various techniques to exert control over the thoughts and actions of party members. These methods often involve restricting access to alternative information sources, encouraging conformity of thought through groupthink, and cultivating an atmosphere characterized by fear and loyalty. Such situations will have significant consequences for democracy, individual freedom, and political discourse, as they often prioritize the leader's interests over the collective well-being and democratic principles.

#

The partial transformation of a political party into

a cult is a complex and nuanced process that cannot be described in a linear fashion. Its intensity and manifestation may vary significantly. However, as of mid-2023, an examination of the Republican Party's political ideology and governance approach reveals a lack of conceptual understanding. While the party identifies as conservative and espouses a range of principles such as limited government intervention, free-market capitalism, individual liberties, and traditional values, their "small government" stance implies a belief in minimal state involvement in the economy, society, and individual lives.

Regrettably, the Republican Party often appears

to overlook the potential long-term consequences and challenges associated with its small government approach. This myopic perspective is reflected in its governance and policymaking processes, which tend to prioritize immediate or short-term goals without adequately considering broader societal implications. The party's emphasis on limited government intervention, while promoting individual freedom and economic prosperity in the short run, raises concerns about its ability to address complex issues and effectively plan.

Critics argue that this narrow-sighted focus on immediate goals and short-term benefits may hinder the Republican Party's ability to tackle multifaceted challenges. By failing to fully grasp the potential long-term implications of their approach, they risk underestimating the complexities and potential obstacles that may arise. This critique underscores the need for the party to broaden its perspective, incorporate a more forward-thinking outlook, and engage in comprehensive long-term planning to navigate complex societal issues effectively.

#

Individuals across the diverse spectrum of political ideologies hold differing views on whether naming misinformation is an act of silencing conservative voices. This belief does not align with the wide range of political ideologies that exist, which can vary in their emphasis on personal freedom, equality, social justice, economic policies, cultural values, and the relationship between the state and its citizens. It is important to recognize that within political discourse, perspectives on the relationship between information accuracy and political voices can differ greatly. Engaging in open and respectful discussions can help foster a deeper understanding of these complex dynamics and the diverse viewpoints within the political landscape.

The goal of showing misinformation is to promote correct and reliable information, regardless of political affiliation. Misinformation can be detrimental to public discourse and decision-making, as it spreads false or misleading narratives that can influence public opinion and shape policies.

However, it is crucial to acknowledge that the feeling of bias or silence can arise when the process of identifying and combating misinformation executed lacks transparency, fairness, and equal scrutiny across different political viewpoints. If there is a belief that fact-checking or content moderation disproportionately targets conservative voices, it can fuel the belief that there is an intentional effort to stifle conservative perspectives.

Addressing this concern requires a commitment to impartiality and ensuring that the identification of misinformation is conducted objectively, with rigorous standards applied consistently to all political ideologies. It is essential to have diverse perspectives involved in the fact-checking and content moderation process to minimize the risk of bias.

Furthermore, efforts to combat misinformation should be coupled with initiatives that promote media literacy and critical thinking skills among the public. By equipping individuals with the ability to discern credible information from misinformation, it becomes less likely that any particular political ideology will be silenced. Encouraging open dialogue, respectful discussions, and a diversity of voices can foster a healthier information ecosystem where misinformation is challenged without suppressing legitimate conservative viewpoints.

#

Fortunately for society, in the relentless march of progress, technology will inevitably outstrip the capabilities of governments, political parties, and individual political agendas, primarily due to its capacity to provide unparalleled transparency and accessibility to the public.

As technological advancements surge forward, they democratize information, breaking down the barriers that once hindered public access to crucial data. The widespread dissemination of information through the internet and other technological channels empowers citizens with real-time updates and comprehensive insights into governmental actions, policies, and decisions.

With this increased transparency, the public can scrutinize the actions of governments and political parties more closely, holding them accountable for their promises and actions. Any attempts to manipulate or obscure information become increasingly challenging in the face of technology's determined gaze. Consequently, political actors are forced to run with a higher degree of integrity and transparency.

Technology also eases communication and networking between citizens, transcending geographical boundaries and creating a global community of informed individuals. People can share their perspectives, concerns, and aspirations, fostering a collective consciousness that transcends traditional political affiliations.

However, as technology advances, it also presents challenges. The pace of technological development may outstrip the ability of policymakers to comprehend and regulate its implications effectively. Privacy concerns, misinformation, and cyber threats become complex issues that demand thoughtful responses and agile governance.

Nevertheless, the overall trajectory shows that technology will continue to shift the balance of power in favor of the public by promoting transparency and open discourse. Governments and political entities will be compelled to adapt to this new reality or risk losing relevance and legitimacy in the eyes of an increasingly tech-savvy and empowered populace. Embracing technology and using it as a tool to foster participatory democracy and inclusivity will be crucial in ensuring a harmonious relationship between governance and technological progress. In this evolving landscape, harnessing the potential of technology for the collective benefit is key to shaping a more accountable, responsive, and transparent political ecosystem.

Politicians who can harness the power of social media, data analytics, and online platforms are better positioned to engage with their constituents, understand their concerns, and tailor policies that resonate with them. As new generations enter the electorate, their tech-savvy nature will become even more pronounced. Younger voters are likely to prioritize candidates who show an understanding of their digital world and use technology to drive positive change. This trend will further challenge politicians who are resistant to technological advancements and hinder their chances of re-election. However, the peril does not end with the retirement of technologically lagging politicians. The arrival of a tech-savvy generation in politics also presents challenges. While being tech-savvy can bring new opportunities for innovative governance and citizen engagement, it also comes with its own set of risks. The speed of information dissemination through social media can lead to misinformation and polarization. Navigating these challenges and ensuring responsible and ethical use of technology in politics is a must. Technology can indeed lead to the expiration of time in office for politicians who fail to keep up with its advancements and benefits. The arrival of a tech-savvy generation in politics will further emphasize the importance of embracing technology for effective governance. However, challenges related to misinformation and responsible use of technology are critical aspects of the digital age. Tackling these challenges requires collaborative efforts among governments, tech companies, civil society, and individuals.

POLITICAL POLARIZATION

As we approach the first quarter of the 21st century, it is truly astonishing that the United States remains deeply entrenched in a conflict between its binary political ideologies and partisan affiliations. This ongoing struggle illustrates the dynamic nature of US politics and how it has evolved as a republic. Despite facing new challenges, the country's political landscape will undoubtedly continue to adapt and transform over time.

The clash of these political stances, with each advocating its own aims, has resulted in the creation of a highly polarized political landscape within the nation. Consequently, stark divisions have appeared along partisan lines, impeded constructive political engagement and pushed voters to strongly align themselves with one of the major political parties. Consequently, issues that further deepen the divides between these parties become the focal point of public discussions.

This heightened polarization is fueled by influential factions within the political elite, which exert an outsized impact on the entire political system. Unfortunately, a considerable number of

Americans currently harbor feelings of anger and an unwillingness to find common ground or compromise, worsening the situation further.

This internal threat to our democracy did not begin ten years ago, but dates back more than two hundred years, 1812 to be exact, the practice of gerrymandering itself may not be the sole cause of political polarization in the United States, but it can be linked to the genesis of the divergence of political attitudes away from the center. This division of a country's entire population into two diametrically opposed political camps can damage our nation's long-term interests. Though slow, the swaying crawl of the salamander for the last two centuries has systematically diluted the voting power of the opposition and gained considerable ground to prove itself as a political force, friend, and foe as its path undulates left and right. While this practice is not the sole cause of political polarization, it can contribute to an environment that reinforces and intensifies existing divisions. The distortion of electoral districts can limit competitive elections, suppress minority voices, create partisan echo chambers, and incentivize extremism. Addressing gerrymandering is one of the steps that can be taken to mitigate political polarization and promote a more inclusive and representative democracy. Promoting transparency in the gerrymandering process is of paramount importance. One effective step is the creation of independent redistricting commissions, composed of non-partisan members, to ensure the fair and unbiased drawing of district boundaries. By involving the public and supplying access to information, we can shine a light on this issue. Transparency and public input become vital tools in mitigating the severe consequences of gerrymandering, allowing us to find and rectify instances of extreme partisan manipulation. Ultimately, making gerrymandering more transparent empowers citizens to hold those responsible accountable and strengthens the foundations of a truly representative democracy.

Making the redistricting process transparent and accessible to the public is essential. Allowing citizens to supply input and feedback on proposed district maps can help prevent manipulation and foster greater public trust in the electoral process.

Apart from gerrymandering, several other crucial factors have played a significant role in the polarization seen in recent years within US politics.

The phenomenon known as "Ideological Sorting" is the process by which individuals and elected officials align themselves with political parties based on their ideological beliefs. As time has passed, the two major political parties, the

Democrats, and the Republicans, have become more ideologically uniform. This trend has resulted in a decline in the number of moderates within each party, leading to a more polarized political landscape. Consequently, there is now a considerable divide between the parties on various policy issues.

This ideological sorting has intensified due to a combination of factors, including partisan alignment, demographic shifts, policy positions, geographic sorting, and polarization over time. As a result, there is a shrinking middle ground for compromise and collaboration, which contributes to the current state of political polarization we see today.

Understanding the phenomenon of ideological sorting is crucial to understanding the dynamics of political polarization. It highlights how individuals and elected officials align themselves with parties based on their ideological beliefs, leading to greater divisions between the parties and reduced opportunities for bipartisan cooperation.

Another common and contributing factor is media fragmentation, this refers to the proliferation of various media sources and platforms, resulting in a diverse and fragmented media landscape. The proliferation of media outlets and the rise of social media have created echo chambers and filter bubbles, where individuals can easily access news and information that align with their existing beliefs. This has led to the reinforcement of partisan viewpoints, as people are less exposed to diverse perspectives and more likely to consume ideologically biased news.

The influence of Cable News and Partisan Outlets is immeasurable as they often or regularly present news with a particular partisan bias, attracting viewers who seek confirmation of their existing beliefs. Online News and social media, the advent of the internet and social media platforms has dramatically increased access to news and information, they have also expanded the range of voices and perspectives available, it has also led to the formation of filter bubbles and echo chambers. The decline of Traditional Media such as newspapers and network news, has experienced a decline in readership and viewership.

Media fragmentation plays a significant role in political polarization by reinforcing partisan identities, limiting exposure to diverse perspectives, and contributing to the spread of misinformation and disinformation. Addressing media fragmentation requires promoting media literacy, encouraging critical thinking, and fostering a diverse and inclusive media ecosystem that supplies balanced and objective reporting.

The use of political rhetoric by leaders and influential figures can contribute to the polarization witnessed in US politics. When these leaders adopt divisive language, resort to personal attacks, or employ inflammatory rhetoric, it deepens the divide between parties and their respective supporters. Polarizing leaders set the tone for their followers, thereby contributing to the overall political polarization.

Furthermore, identity-based issues like race, gender, religion, and sexual orientation have become major points of contention in the political arena. Political parties and interest groups often mobilize their bases by framing debates around these identity-based topics, which intensifies polarization on social and cultural fronts. This creates a feedback loop where politicians cater to their base's more extreme demands to secure electoral victories, and voters, in turn, become more entrenched in their partisan identities. As this cycle perpetuates, it becomes increasingly challenging for politicians to bridge the gap and find common ground across party lines.

While the primary election process serves as a crucial mechanism for selecting political candidates in democratic systems, it is not without its drawbacks. For one the lack of representativeness as primaries tends to have a lower turnout compared to general elections, hence, the candidate choice may not fully reflect the preference and diversity of the broader electorate. The primary process can be influenced by well-funded interest groups or wealthy individuals who may support specific candidates. This process often attracts more ideologically extreme or partisan voters, which can contribute to the nomination of candidates who hold more extreme positions.

Primaries tend to attract more ideologically extreme voters, as they are more likely to take part in the candidate selection process. As a result, candidates who win primaries may be more ideologically rigid, which further reinforces the partisan divide. It is important to note that these factors are interconnected and can reinforce one another, creating a complex web of polarization in US politics. Addressing these issues and promoting more inclusive, open-minded dialogue is crucial to mitigating polarization and fostering a healthier political climate.

Political polarization has led to increased partisan gridlock and legislative inefficiency. With deep divisions between political parties, it becomes challenging to pass legislation and make substantial progress on critical issues. The focus often shifts from finding common ground and working collaboratively to advancing partisan agendas, leading to legislative stalemates and a lack of meaningful policy solutions.

This increasing ideological distance and division between different political groups has eroded public trust in political institutions and leaders. As the political climate becomes more polarized, people are more likely to view the opposing party and its supporters as a threat to their values and interests. This leads to heightened distrust and animosity, undermining the foundations of democratic governance. Additionally, polarization can discourage civic engagement, as individuals may feel disillusioned or disengaged from a system they perceive as divisive and unresponsive. Furthermore, it has made it increasingly difficult to achieve compromise and foster bipartisanship. The willingness to work across party lines and find common ground has diminished, resulting in a more confrontational and partisan political landscape. This makes it challenging to address complex challenges effectively, as policy decisions often become ideological battlegrounds rather than opportunities for collaboration and negotiation.

Polarization can strain democratic institutions and undermine their effectiveness. When partisan interests take precedence over the broader principles of democracy, there is a risk of institutional erosion and a breakdown in checks and balances. This can have long-term consequences for the separation of powers, the rule of law, and the functioning of democratic systems. Such has been amplified by the rise of social media and the proliferation of echo chambers.

Individuals are increasingly exposed to like-minded individuals and sources of information that reinforce their existing beliefs, further polarizing society. This can lead to the spread of misinformation, making it challenging for citizens to make informed decisions and engage in constructive political discourse.

When polarization dominates the political

landscape, the focus tends to shift away from policy innovation and problem-solving. Instead of developing innovative and evidence-based solutions, the emphasis often lies in defending partisan positions and scoring political points. This hampers the ability to address emerging challenges effectively and adapt to a rapidly changing world.

Americans are showing a decreasing tolerance for extreme rhetoric and divisive language from political leaders. There is an increasing demand for leaders who promote civil discourse and engage in respectful dialogue, rather than engaging in inflammatory or polarizing rhetoric.

However, it is important to note that political

polarization still is a significant challenge, and its effects are still deeply entrenched in the political landscape. While there may be a growing awareness and desire for change, overcoming polarization requires sustained efforts at various levels of society, including political leaders, media organizations, and grassroots initiatives.

#

Today, we find ourselves at a critical juncture in the history of our great nation. It is a time when political polarization has reached unprecedented heights, creating deep chasms that threaten the very fabric of our society. Political polarization has led to a breakdown in constructive dialogue. Instead of engaging in civil conversations, we find ourselves entangled in bitter disputes, where opposing viewpoints are treated as adversaries rather than opportunities for growth.

We must recognize that diversity of thought is the hallmark of a healthy democracy, which is the foundation on how our nation was built. However, when this diversity transforms into divisiveness, we lose sight of the principles that have made us strong, we become weaker as a nation when we forsake the values of respect, empathy, and compromise. The responsibility to heal our nation does not rest solely on the shoulders of our leaders; it falls upon each one of us. We, the citizens, have the power to change the course of our nation's future. It begins with acknowledging that our fellow Americans, regardless of their political affiliation, are not enemies but allies in the pursuit of a better tomorrow.

Let us commit ourselves to promoting open and respectful dialogue. Instead of retreating to the comfort of echo chambers, let us embrace conversations that challenge our beliefs. In doing so, we can learn from each other and find common ground, however small it may seem.

Furthermore, we must demand accountability from our elected officials. Leaders who prioritize political point-scoring over the welfare of the nation must be held answerable.

Let us celebrate those who transcend party lines, who show the courage to work collaboratively, and who prioritize the needs of the people. We must reject the notion that compromise equates to weakness. Instead, let us embrace the idea that reaching across the aisle and finding common solutions proves strength, resilience, and a commitment to progress. Together, we can build a stronger, more united nation. It requires courage, empathy, and a shared vision for a better future. The challenges before us are great, but so is our collective potential to overcome them.

The concept of the right to privacy encompasses the fundamental idea that individuals have the inherent right to be free from unwarranted intrusion or interference into their personal lives, decisions, and private affairs. While the phrase "right to privacy" is not explicitly mentioned in the United States Constitution, it has been acknowledged and safeguarded by the Supreme

Court through its interpretation of various

constitutional provisions.

Over time, the understanding and scope of

the right to privacy have evolved through

significant rulings by the Supreme Court, one of the

most notable being Roe v. Wade in 1973. This

groundbreaking decision established the

constitutional right to abortion and affirmed a

woman's right to choose without excessive

government interference, grounded in the

constitutional right to privacy.

However, in recent years, there has been a

worrisome trend among Supreme Court Justices to

overturn earlier decisions rather than making progressive rulings that align with the advancements of society. This raises concerns about the consequences of a Supreme Court ruling that overturns or weakens the constitutional protection for abortion. Such a development will have far-reaching implications for civil rights, American democracy, law, and policy. In a nation deeply divided, interpreting, and applying the "law of the land" requires a comprehensive understanding of the diverse philosophical perspectives and approaches to the law within society. It needs grappling with the intricacies of legal reasoning, precedent, and societal transformations while striving to keep the stability, fairness, and legitimacy of the judicial and legal system. The stark disparity between the overwhelming support for the right to abortion, with over sixty percent of the U.S. population in favor, and the actions of politicians highlights a palpable disconnect between elected officials and the desires of their constituents. This disconnect is most profoundly rooted in Washington DC but is also clear in state capitals and even in the myriad of incorporated municipalities, towns, and villages across the nation.

The reversal of Roe v. Wade disregards the profound implications it holds for women's autonomy and overlooks the societal progress that has reinforced the rights affirmed in this landmark ruling. The right to choose is not solely about the legality of abortion but is deeply entwined with gender equality and women's empowerment.

By invalidating the core principles upheld in Roe v. Wade, the Court does not recognize the fundamental right of women to make decisions about their own bodies and reproductive health. It dismisses the strides made towards gender equality and the recognition of women as autonomous individuals capable of making informed choices about their lives.

Over the course of fifty years, the landmark decision of Roe v. Wade has undeniably had a profound impact on two successive societal generations, leading them to adopt and embrace the principles enshrined in this historic ruling. It has come to recognize that access to safe and legal abortion is essential for women to exercise control over their futures, pursue education and careers, and fully take part in society on equal terms with men. Denying women, the right to choose denies them the ability to shape their own destinies and

perpetuates gender inequality.

Furthermore, privacy plays a crucial role in

empowering individuals to associate freely, form

communities, and engage in private gatherings

without unwarranted interference or surveillance. It

fosters the development of social and political

groups that are integral to a thriving civil society.

By safeguarding an individual's innermost

thoughts, beliefs, and religious practices from

unwanted scrutiny, privacy enables the exploration

of personal convictions and upholds the right to

freedom of thought and religion, without the fear of

judgment or persecution.

Privacy also assumes a vital role in protecting

marginalized and vulnerable populations from

unjustified scrutiny and discrimination. It acts as a

shield, safeguarding personal information that, if

exposed, could be weaponized to target individuals

based on their race, ethnicity, gender, sexuality, or

other protected characteristics. By preserving this

information, privacy mitigates the potential for

systemic bias, prejudice, and unwarranted harm.

Moreover, privacy serves as a catalyst for

individual autonomy, easing self-expression and

personal growth. It reinforces the principles of equality and dignity by ensuring that every person, irrespective of their background or identity, has the freedom to associate, develop their beliefs, and share intimate aspects of their lives with confidence. Upholding privacy rights is indispensable in constructing a just and inclusive society that respects and embraces the diversity and individuality of its members.

While privacy rights are crucial for all individuals, it is important to acknowledge that certain factors can disproportionately affect women's privacy and contribute to gender inequality. The issue of women's inequality has seen a concerning rise, particularly in relation to privacy rights. Women's reproductive choices, such as contraception and abortion, have become battlefields for intense debates and tries to restrict access. These debates often encroach upon women's privacy and autonomy, subjecting personal decisions about their bodies and reproductive health to external scrutiny and regulation. Such intrusions undermine women's rights and perpetuate gender inequality.

Moreover, women from marginalized communities face intersecting challenges that compound privacy concerns. Factors such as race,

ethnicity, socioeconomic status, or immigration

status intersect with gender, resulting in

discrimination, surveillance, and privacy violations

that target multiple dimensions of their identity.

These compound challenges intensify the impact on

their lives and limit their opportunities, further

deepening gender inequality.

Additionally, the workplace becomes another

arena where women's privacy is compromised,

contributing to ongoing disparities. Unequal

treatment, pay gaps, and intrusive practices

undermine women's autonomy and reinforce

gender-based discrimination. Women meet obstacles in achieving professional success due to gender bias, harassment, and privacy violations within professional environments. These infringements perpetuate a climate of inequality, hindering women's advancement and reinforcing systemic gender-based disparities.

Women often find themselves facing the difficult decision of abortion due to distinct reasons, including insufficient income or lack of financial support to support the basic needs of a child. These needs encompass vital aspects such as food, clothing, shelter, healthcare, and education. The absence of affordable housing is a major contributing factor that can have severe consequences for single mothers and their children. It can lead to unstable living situations, overcrowding, or even homelessness, negatively affecting their overall well-being and stability. Let us not forget to include discrimination based on familial status as it is an unfortunate reality in the housing market. Some landlords or property owners may be hesitant to rent to single mothers, fearing that they may struggle to pay rent or keep the property adequately. Furthermore, living in substandard housing can pose health and safety risks, affecting the physical and emotional health of both the mother and her children. This happens as they grapple with the challenge of securing reliable and affordable childcare options, such as daycare centers, babysitters, or after-school programs, to ensure the child's safety and supervision while the mother is occupied with work or other responsibilities.

The limited access to healthcare and health insurance coverage adds to the concerns of ensuring the child's medical needs are adequately met. Nonetheless, scarce resources for the child's educational development and limited opportunities for learning, such as access to books, educational toys, quality schools, or educational programs, further compound the difficulties faced by women contemplating their options.

Meeting the child's nutritional requirements and providing a balanced and nutritious diet becomes a struggle without the means to plan meals, buy groceries, and prepare healthy food at home. Moreover, the inability to create a safe and secure home environment for the child poses added challenges, including childproofing the house, installing safety measures, and keeping cleanliness.

Transportation presents yet another obstacle, as lacking reliable options such as a car or access to public transportation hinders the ability to meet the

child's needs, including commuting to school,

attending medical appointments, and taking part in

extracurricular activities.

These multifaceted issues contribute to the

complexities that women face when considering

abortion, highlighting the significant socioeconomic

factors that influence their decision-making process.

It is important to acknowledge and address these

challenges when denying women, the given right to

choose.

As society changes, so do the values and

norms that influence public opinion and policy. The

Court's composition, which can remain unchanged

for decades due to lifetime tenure, lags societal

shifts, leading to decisions that are inconsistent or

out of touch with contemporary views.

Addressing the increasing inequality faced by

women needs comprehensive and targeted action. It

requires challenging restrictive policies

surrounding reproductive choices, ensuring access

to comprehensive healthcare services, and

safeguarding women's privacy rights. Efforts must

be made to dismantle barriers that intersect with

gender, such as racism, socioeconomic disparities,

and immigration status. Promoting inclusive and

respectful workplaces, free from discrimination and privacy violations, is crucial to empowering women and creating a fairer society.

The right to privacy is a fundamental aspect of individual freedom and autonomy. It encompasses the protection of personal lives, decisions, and private affairs from unwarranted intrusion or interference. Although the specific phrase "right to privacy" is not explicitly said in the United States Constitution, the Supreme Court has acknowledged and upheld this right through its interpretation of constitutional provisions. The Supreme Court's recent inclination towards overturning precedent instead of issuing progressive rulings has sparked apprehension over the potential ramifications of undermining constitutional protection. Notably, this trend raises concerns not only for abortion rights but also for fundamental freedoms such as freedom of speech and voting rights, among others. The Court's perceived ineffectiveness in upholding crucial constitutional principles has become a topic of significant worry. This could have far-reaching implications for civil rights, American democracy, law, and policy.

Upholding or protecting the right to choose is essential not only for women but also for promoting equality, health, and the well-being of individuals and society. It is a fundamental aspect of human rights and individual freedom that should be safeguarded and respected.

Additionally, privacy plays a critical role in easing freedom of association, protecting marginalized populations, and fostering individual autonomy. Addressing the inequalities faced by women requires comprehensive action to challenge restrictive policies, ensure access to healthcare services, and safeguard privacy rights. By doing so, we can work towards a more just and inclusive society that respects and embraces the diversity of its members.

#

The US Constitution primarily focuses on the rights and protections afforded to living persons. However, it does supply a framework for the interpretation and application of rights that can extend to various aspects of individuals' lives, including privacy. The historical interpretation of the term "person" in the Constitution has consistently referred to individuals who are already born. As a result, it was widely understood that the constitutional rights protected by the 14th

Amendment were granted only upon a person's live

birth. This understanding, however, calls into

question the recognition of women's right to choose

on their reproductive decisions and the status of an

unborn person.

The ongoing debate surrounding the right to

choose centers on a woman's autonomy and

decision-making power over her own body, that

this fundamental right extends to a woman's right

to make choices about her pregnancy, including

whether to continue or end it. Restrictions on

abortion, which limit a woman's ability to exercise

her reproductive rights, infringe upon her personal autonomy and violate her constitutional rights. Constitutionally, a woman's right to make choices about her own body should take precedence over potential rights attributed to an unborn person. Granting full constitutional rights to the unborn could undermine a woman's autonomy, jeopardize her health, and restrict her access to necessary reproductive healthcare.

#

To decide whether the conceptus or fetus should be recognized as constitutional persons, as such let's help congress regain some credibility and ask of them to consider the implementation of a constitutional amendment, rather than relying solely on court rulings that are susceptible to interpretation and modification instead of continue using this right to privacy as political agenda.

The question at hand pertains to bestowing or not constitutional personhood upon the conceptus or fetus. This issue is significant as it involves the fundamental legal rights and protections that are granted to individuals under the constitution. To address this matter comprehensively, a constitutional amendment would be the most proper course of action.

Relying solely on court decisions to set up the constitutional personhood of the conceptus or fetus poses several challenges. Court rulings can be subject to interpretation, and their interpretations may evolve over time due to changes in judicial philosophy or societal attitudes. As a result, the legal status and protections granted to the conceptus or fetus might be uncertain or prone to alteration.

In comparison, a constitutional amendment gives a lasting and definite solution. To amend the constitution, a deliberate and structured process is needed. In this case, it should involve input from medical experts, the public, and the usual

contributions from various government agencies

and branches. This ensures a comprehensive

examination of the issue and allows for the

establishment of clear and unambiguous criteria for

granting constitutional personhood.

By pursuing a constitutional amendment, the

intention is to provide a stable and lasting legal

framework that defines the conceptus or fetus as

constitutional persons or not, with all the attendant

rights and protections. This approach removes the

reliance on potentially fluctuating court decisions,

ensuring a consistent and reliable standard for deciding the legal status of the conceptus or fetus.

In conclusion, recognizing the conceptus or fetus as constitutional persons needs the adoption of a constitutional amendment, which offers a more steadfast and definitive approach compared to relying solely on court rulings. This would ensure that the determination of constitutional personhood is still consistent, clear, and enduring.

#

Raising a child is an incredibly rewarding yet undeniably challenging journey. The demands placed on single mothers go well beyond the limited perspective ingrained in societal norms.

These norms, which are shaped by the prevailing

values, beliefs, and expectations of a society, often

perpetuate stereotypes, bias, and unfair treatment.

However, what is even more concerning is the

glaring disconnect between the progress of societies

and the unwillingness of elected officials to adapt to

new norms.

Societies are constantly evolving, responding

to social and cultural shifts. Norms and values

change over time, and societies strive to become

more inclusive, diverse, and progressive.

Unfortunately, elected officials often do not

recognize and embrace these changes. Influenced by traditional beliefs, political ideologies, or a desire to keep the status quo, they often lag in responding to the evolving needs and aspirations of the society they are supposed to serve. This disconnection creates a significant gap in representation and responsiveness.

A major factor worsening this issue is the generational divide. Societies are composed of diverse age groups, each with their own unique perspectives, values, and expectations. Younger generations, with their enthusiasm for social change, often lead the charge in driving new norms and ideas. However, elected officials, who tend to be older and from earlier generations, struggle to understand and relate to the aspirations and priorities of younger citizens. This disconnect further widens the gap between societal progress and the policies and decisions made by those in power.

The unwillingness of elected officials to adapt to new norms is a significant roadblock to progress. Political pressures, the fear of backlash from certain segments of society, and personal biases often contribute to their resistance to change. Unfortunately, this resistance hinders progress and stifles the responsiveness needed to address

emerging issues and concerns effectively.

To bridge this gap, it is essential to foster a

more dynamic and inclusive political landscape.

Encouraging greater diversity in political

representation can help ensure that a wider range of

perspectives is considered in decision-making

processes. Transparency and accountability

mechanisms must be strengthened to hold elected

officials responsible for their actions. Additionally,

creating platforms for meaningful public

participation in policy discussions can help bridge

the divide between elected officials and the

evolving aspirations of society.

It is crucial for governments to recognize the

imperative of adapting to new norms to effectively

serve their constituents. The world is rapidly

changing, and societies are evolving at an

unprecedented pace. Elected officials must shed

their unwillingness to change, actively engage with

shifting social and cultural dynamics, and embrace

progressive values. Only then can they truly stand

for the interests and needs of the people they are

elected to serve. By doing so, we can foster a more

inclusive and responsive government that keeps

pace with the ever-evolving society it stands for.

WOKE

"Woke" - an adjective, chiefly US slang - refers
to being aware and actively attentive to important
societal facts and issues, particularly those
concerning racial and social justice. This definition
can be found on merriam-webster.com.

The modern usage of the term "woke" can be
traced back to African American Vernacular English
(AAVE) in the mid-20th century. In the AAVE
context, being "woke" held the significance of being

conscious of and actively confronting racial injustice and systemic oppression. However, in the 2010s, the term experienced a resurgence in popularity, becoming linked to a broader social and political movement centered around social justice and progressive activism. Today, "woke" is a powerful and influential force, motivating individuals and groups to advocate for positive change and a more equitable society.

The modern "woke" movement has deep historical roots that can be traced back to several key factors that shaped its development over time. One of the pivotal influences was the Civil Rights

Movement that took place in the United States during the 1950s and 1960s. This transformative period of activism and resistance against racial segregation and discrimination had a profound impact on inspiring a sense of social consciousness about racial inequality and injustice. The Civil Rights Movement not only sought to secure equal rights and opportunities for African Americans but also paved the way for broader movements advocating for justice and equality for marginalized communities.

The legacy of the Civil Rights Movement extended into the subsequent decades and contributed to the rise of identity politics in the 1970s and 1980s. Identity politics emphasized the significance of recognizing and addressing the unique challenges faced by different social groups based on their identities, which included race, gender, sexual orientation, and more. It urged individuals to be aware of the experiences and struggles of others and to work collectively toward dismantling systems of oppression that perpetuated inequality.

As society became more attuned to the intricacies of identity politics, it laid the groundwork for the revival of the "woke" movement in the 2010s. This resurgence was driven by a younger generation that used social media platforms to raise awareness about social justice issues, mobilize collective action, and challenge the status quo. The term "woke" took on a new meaning, encompassing a broader spectrum of progressive ideals and actions aimed at combating various forms of discrimination and advocating for inclusivity and equity.

With its historical roots in the Civil Rights Movement and its evolution through identity politics, the modern "woke" movement has become a powerful force for societal change. It has fostered a growing awareness of systemic inequalities and injustices while encouraging individuals to critically engage with social issues and contribute to positive transformation. The "woke" movement continues to evolve and adapt to contemporary challenges, proving its enduring relevance in the pursuit of a more just and equitable world.

More recently, the advent of social media and the internet supplied a platform for marginalized voices and allowed information about existing social injustices to spread widely and rapidly. This enabled social justice movements to gain visibility and mobilize supporters globally.

In politics the term "woke" transcends party lines, serving as a concise expression of political progressiveness among the left, while being employed by the right to criticize leftist culture. The term "woke" is not self-evident to everyone, as its meaning can vary depending on the context and the perspective of the person using it. While a diverse number of individuals may be familiar with its usage to refer to heightened awareness of social issues, others might not be acquainted with its specific connotations and associations with political and social progressiveness. Therefore, its understanding may require some context or explanation in certain situations.

There are conservative individuals and Republicans who criticize the concept of "wokeness" and how it applies in society. They argue that the ideas associated with being "woke" can sometimes lead to what they perceive as excessive political correctness, cancel culture, and a dismissal of differing viewpoints.

The term "woke" has been used in an array of ways, and some critics argue that it can be used as a divisional tool by politicians or other groups to polarize and manipulate public opinion. The term is associated with progressive or socially aware ideologies, while some politicians or political commentators may use it to discredit or criticize

certain social or political movements, portraying

them as overly sensitive or extreme.

On the other hand, proponents of social

justice and progressive movements see the term

"woke" as a positive attribute, standing for

increased awareness and empathy towards social

issues. They view it as an essential tool for

promoting inclusivity and equality.

Similarly with many political terms, its usage

can be subject to manipulation and polarization

depending on the context and the intentions of

those using it. It is important to critically evaluate

how any term is used in political discourse and understand the diverse perspectives surrounding it. It is essential to be aware of manipulative tactics like gaslighting and to critically evaluate political rhetoric to understand the intentions behind it, as many do not shy away from exploiting the language of social justice or activism to manipulate and deceive others for their own ideological agenda.

The voter's resistance against polarizing speech has sparked a surge of progressive political activism that extends well beyond the realm of politics. Ordinary Americans, especially young individuals who previously saw themselves as apolitical, are now passionately involved in political discussions, marking their first-time hyper-engagement in such matters.

#

In the ever-evolving political landscape, the term "woke" has taken on a multifaceted meaning that extends beyond being associated with a singular political party. It has evolved into a broader social and cultural movement, encompassing a range of progressive ideas and issues that resonate with various segments of society. This expansion has led politicians and political groups to both embrace "woke" issues and incorporate them into their platforms, as well as criticize the concept to appeal to their respective bases or target specific demographics.

On one hand, certain politicians and political groups have recognized the growing influence of the "woke" movement and its alignment with the values and concerns of certain constituencies. In response, they have embraced and championed "woke" issues to appeal to progressive voters and garner support from communities that prioritize social justice, equity, and inclusivity. By incorporating these issues into their platforms, politicians look to position themselves as advocates

for positive change and social progress, tapping

into the energy and passion of the "woke"

movement to mobilize their base.

On the other hand, there are politicians and

political groups who view the "woke" movement

with skepticism or outright hostility. They may

criticize the concept as being too politically correct,

divisive, or unrealistic in their pursuit of social

change. For these critics, "woke" issues are seen as

potential threats to traditional values and beliefs,

and they use this critique to appeal to their own

base of supporters, which may include more conservative or traditional demographics.

In either case, the rise of the "woke" movement has undoubtedly influenced political discourse and strategies. It has become a rallying point for some and a point of contention for others. As a result, "woke" issues have found their way into public debates, policy discussions, and electoral campaigns, shaping the broader political narrative.

While the "woke" movement has garnered significant attention and influence, it still is a complex and evolving force in politics. As the social and cultural landscape continues to shift, so too will the ways in which politicians and political groups

engage with "woke" issues. In this dynamic

environment, understanding the nuances of the

"woke" movement and its impact on political

dynamics will be crucial for navigating the

complexities of contemporary politics.

In mid-2023, the "woke" movement has

significantly gained momentum, with one-third of

all registered voters in the United States identifying

as "woke." Notably, around sixty percent of

Democrats view "woke" as a positive force, while

thirty-nine percent of Republicans see it as a

negative aspect. Independents also show support

for "woke," with thirty-six percent expressing

favorable views. These statistics show that the

"woke" movement has appeared as a potent

political force, underscoring a clear disconnect

between elected officials and their constituents.

The political landscape in Florida presents an

intriguing opportunity to delve into the

phenomenon of anti-wokeness and its role as a

potential distraction from critical social issues.

Observing the state's ideology and intent on anti-

wokeness, one can discern its use as a deliberate

diversion, crafted within a controlled environment

to minimize the influence of certain significant

factors. This intriguing setup supplies a unique lens to study the impact and implications of such distractions on pressing societal concerns.

While controlled environments are valuable for research purposes, it is crucial to acknowledge their limitations in replicating real-world conditions, especially when examining certain aspects of human behavior, predictability, and characteristics such as individual freedom, autonomy, and self-reliance. These complex sides are challenging to simulate accurately, and we must not underestimate the intricacy of human thought and consciousness.

In the pursuit of expanding their political base and turning extreme ideologies into tangible reality, some have sought an alternative to the mainstream approach. This new platform of extremism, known as "anti-woke," appears with radical and unwavering views that diverge from the center of the political spectrum.

Seeking a way to attract more followers and echoing the fervent loyalty seen in the past, proponents of the anti-woke movement have tried to emulate the strategies of the earlier MAGA (Make America Great Again) movement and its charismatic leader. Though they could not shed their cult-like following, they aimed to achieve similar success by adopting a similar concept and method, giving rise to the anti-woke ideology as a political platform.

Though it is essential to recognize that this belief of past greatness is not universal and often criticized for not considering the experiences of marginalized and oppressed communities throughout history. For many, "America's former greatness" is associated with a time of significant inequality, racial segregation, and limited civil rights for certain groups.

Digging deeper into this matter, it is worth

noting that Florida has experienced uninterrupted

Republican leadership in both the governor's office

and legislature for almost a quarter of a century,

starting from 1999. Throughout this time, they have

adeptly employed the concept of "smoke and

mirrors" to manage and navigate various situations

while staying in elected office. As of 2023, the

unambiguous consequence of relying on deception

is that the state is now confronted with a multitude

of challenges. The consistent use of charlatan

rhetoric has resulted in Florida obtaining the

unfortunate distinction of having the highest

homeowners' insurance rates in the nation. In a

masterful display of smoke and mirrors, the Florida

legislature managed to pass a bill that cleverly

concealed its true impact. Among various

provisions, the bill deceptively "limits applicability

of provisions relating to attorney fees in certain

actions against insurers." While it may appear

harmless at first glance, this cunning move unfairly

shifts the advantage to the insurers, leaving

claimants at a disadvantage and adding insult to

injury. Moreover, Florida ranks among the top five

states with a sizable part of its residents lacking

health insurance, standing at 12.54 percent.

Moreover, Florida's current state of affairs

concerning healthcare is concerning. The state holds

the unfortunate distinction of having the nation's second-highest rate of uninsured residents below the age of 65, totaling approximately 3.8 million individuals. This alarming figure accounts for about 25 percent of the entire state's population, with more than 500,000 of those uninsured being younger than 19, as per U.S. Census data. One of the contributing factors to this issue is a prior legislative decision not to expand federal Medicaid insurance, which has denied access to healthcare for many of the "living poor." Such a stance seems to align with an anti-woke agenda, further exacerbating the problem.

In addition to the healthcare challenges,
Florida faces other financial hurdles. It ranks as the
fourth-highest state in terms of auto insurance costs,
placing a burden on its residents. Furthermore, the
state's household income is ranked 36th in the
nation, indicating lower average incomes among its
population. These factors combine to create a
complex economic situation for many Floridians.

The state's persistent reliance on misleading
tactics to divert attention from critical matters has
had a profound and detrimental impact on its
overall functionality. By employing such methods,
the state has impeded its own progress in

addressing pressing issues effectively. One of the glaring consequences of this unfortunate situation is the ongoing struggle to find practical solutions, particularly clear in the realm of affordable housing.

The persistent challenge of providing affordable housing has plagued Florida, making it one of the least affordable states in the nation. The state's inability to tackle this issue efficiently stems, in part, from the distracting tactics used by its political leaders. As attention is diverted away from essential matters, the focus on finding effective and comprehensive solutions is diluted, perpetuating the problem at hand.

These circumstances offer a glimpse into the intricate and complex challenges arising from the ever-evolving political ideologies and policies within the state. The polarization of political parties has intensified in recent times, leading to increased animosity between Democrats and Republicans. In the past, there might have been instances when the two parties worked together more harmoniously, and ideas from both sides were considered and endorsed. However, the current landscape of heightened partisanship has hindered the cooperative spirit that could foster innovative and comprehensive solutions to the state's issues.

As we reflect on the past and present state of governance, it becomes clear that a more inclusive and collaborative approach is vital to address the challenges facing Florida. By transcending partisan divisions and focusing on the common goal of serving the public's best interests, it becomes possible to navigate the complexities of policymaking more effectively. Only by fostering a culture of open dialogue, constructive debate, and willingness to consider ideas from all perspectives can we hope to create a more prosperous and fair future for the state and its residents.

Unfortunately for the residents, the state's overreliance on misleading tactics, coupled with the increasingly polarized political landscape, has hindered its ability to function optimally.

\#

The party's unyielding drive to achieve political gains, without considering the ramifications of their tumultuous civic performance in serving the public interest, appears to know no limits. Despite the lack of evidence showing voters' disapproval, the party consistently secures re-election, which emboldens them to pursue their agenda even further. This situation has led to a growing focus on passing "anti-woke" legislation, seemingly with ease, without giving due consideration to its potential impact on pressing social issues.

The party's single-minded pursuit of political victories may stem from various factors. Firstly, in today's hyper-partisan political climate, some politicians and parties prioritize maintaining or expanding their power base over addressing the genuine concerns of the public. This can lead to a disconnect between the actions of elected officials and the needs of the constituents they represent.

Secondly, the phenomenon of electoral polarization can contribute to the lack of accountability. If voters are deeply divided along party lines and primarily vote along ideological affiliations, politicians may feel secure in their positions, regardless of their performance or policy choices.

Moreover, the concept of "anti-woke" legislation has emerged as a response to the broader "woke" movement that advocates for social justice and progressive change. This form of legislation is often driven by those who view the "woke" movement as a threat to traditional values and believe it goes too far in addressing societal issues. Consequently, they may see passing such legislation as a way to appeal to their base and solidify their support.

However, the pursuit of "anti-woke" legislation, while politically advantageous for some, may not effectively address the pressing social issues at hand. This approach risks diverting attention from critical challenges that demand genuine and thoughtful solutions. In some cases, it may even worsen existing divisions and hinder progress on vital matters such as inequality, discrimination, and systemic injustice.

Holding politicians accountable for their civic performance and evaluating the impact of their decisions on broader society is crucial in fostering responsible governance.

The party's relentless pursuit of political gains despite their chaotic civic performance poses significant challenges and its palpable in the absence of clear voter disapproval. The focus on passing "anti-woke" legislation may be a symptom of a broader polarization in society and politics.

#

We all should advocate for the natural right of every individual to think freely and turn their thoughts into actions, also let's uphold that freedom

should not be restricted but should come with

accountability for the consequences of one's actions.

While in most democratic societies, freedom of

thought is a fundamental human right, allowing

individuals to hold and express their beliefs,

opinions, and ideas without fear of persecution or

censorship. This freedom is essential for fostering

intellectual diversity, encouraging innovation, and

enabling the exchange of ideas that can lead to

progress. However, it is important to note that

while freedom of thought is a cherished value, the

freedom to act on those thoughts is not without

limitations. Societies usually impose restrictions on

certain actions to protect the rights and well-being of others or to prevent harm to society. These restrictions are typically determined by laws and regulations established through democratic processes.

The concept of accountability is also crucial when discussing freedoms and actions. Accountability means that individuals must take responsibility for the consequences of their actions, especially when those actions negatively affect others or society at large. Balancing individual freedoms with accountability is an ongoing challenge in any society. Striking the right balance ensures that personal liberties are protected while

preventing misuse that could cause harm or

infringe upon the rights of others.

The Supreme Court of the United States was established on September 24, 1789. It was created as part of the Judiciary Act of 1789 and was signed into law by President George Washington. The Court's establishment was mandated by Article III of the United States Constitution, which outlines the structure and powers of the federal judiciary. The Supreme Court is the highest court in the United States and serves as the final arbiter in legal disputes involving federal law, the Constitution, and cases of significant importance.

The Supreme Court, bearing immense responsibility, works as an undemocratic institution devoid of accountability. As such, and time has proven that there is a pressing need to impose limitations on its power, ensuring that this body is answerable to appropriate checks and balances. The question of the unconstitutionality of the United States Supreme Court is a complex and contentious issue, below listed are some founding facts that prove a sound argument meriting consideration for constitutional revision.

For one you can argue that the Supreme Court lacks sufficient mechanisms for accountability. The justices are appointed for life by the President with Senate confirmation, which means they can serve for decades without facing re-election or the need to answer to the public. This lifetime tenure may undermine the principle of checks and balances, as it insulates the justices from public opinion and democratic scrutiny.

The interpretation of the Constitution by the court has ignited significant debate, primarily centered around the extent to which certain rulings by the Supreme Court have exceeded its constitutional authority. This controversy stems from the divergence between two prominent approaches to constitutional interpretation: judicial activism and originalism. These contrasting perspectives continue to fuel lively discussions within legal and academic circles.

Some critics argue that justices have engaged in judicial activism, a practice where they impose their personal policy preferences rather than adhering strictly to the original intent or text of the Constitution. Judicial activism can have detrimental effects on the democratic process and encroach upon the power of the legislative branch. Judicial activism refers to a judicial approach in which judges are more inclined to interpret the law creatively, expand constitutional rights, and make policy decisions rather than strictly adhering to the original intent of the legislature or constitution.

The critics' concern stems from the belief that judges, who are not directly elected by the people, should not have the authority to make decisions that affect the legislative process. They argue that this kind of activism can undermine democratic principles by allowing unelected judges to wield significant influence over public policy and social issues. As such many contend that such decisions should be left to the elected representatives who are accountable to the electorate.

One of the pillars of democracy is the separation of powers, which divides authority among the three branches of government: the executive, legislative, and judicial branches. The legislative branch, made up of elected representatives, is responsible for making laws, while the judicial branch's role is to interpret and apply those laws. Critics of judicial activism argue that when judges overstep their role by making policy decisions, they intrude upon the legislative function, blurring the separation of powers.

Moreover, critics assert that judicial activism can undermine the democratic process by circumventing the will of the people. In a representative democracy, the legislature reflects the will of the electorate through the democratic process of electing representatives. By making policy decisions, judges may be imposing their own subjective views on societal matters, potentially disregarding the preferences of the majority, or overriding the decisions made by elected officials. This can be seen as an erosion of democratic accountability and the principle of majority rule.

One can also argue that judicial activism will lead to uncertainty and inconsistency in the law. When judges make policy decisions that go beyond the original intent of the legislature, it can create a lack of predictability in the legal system. This unpredictability can have negative implications for individuals, businesses, and the overall functioning of society.

In summary, many believe that judicial activism can undermine the democratic process and encroach upon legislative power by allowing unelected judges to make policy decisions and potentially override the will of the people. They argue that this can lead to a blurring of the separation of powers, a disregard for democratic accountability, and a lack of predictability in the legal system.

Moreover, critics of judicial activism contend that this approach can undermine the democratic process. When judges go beyond the original intent or text of the Constitution, they effectively bypass the will of the people and their elected representatives. By relying on their own policy preferences, justices may make decisions that are not in alignment with the values and priorities of the society they serve. This can lead to a sense of judicial overreach and diminish public trust in the

courts as impartial arbiters of justice.

In contrast to judicial activism, originalism is

an approach to constitutional interpretation that

emphasizes adhering to the original intent or

understanding of the Constitution at the time it was

written. Originalists argue that the Constitution's

meaning is fixed and can only be changed through

formal amendment processes. They contend that

the role of judges is to interpret the law based on its

original meaning, rather than injecting their own

subjective judgments. Originalism looks to limit

judicial discretion and promote stability in constitutional interpretation.

However, originalism is not without its own criticisms. Opponents argue that the original intent or understanding of the Constitution can be difficult to discern, given the inherent ambiguities in language and the complexity of historical context. They contend that relying solely on the framers' intent may overlook societal advancements and not address contemporary issues adequately. Critics of originalism argue that it can lead to rigid interpretations that hinder progress and deny constitutional protections to marginalized groups.

In conclusion, the debates surrounding judicial activism and originalism reflect differing perspectives on the proper role of judges in interpreting the Constitution. While judicial activism allows for a dynamic and evolving interpretation of the Constitution, it also raises concerns about judicial overreach and the erosion of democratic principles. On the other hand, originalism looks to keep fidelity to the framers' intent but can be criticized for its potential rigidity and limited adaptability. Achieving a balance between these contrasting approaches is still an ongoing challenge in constitutional law and requires careful consideration of the values, principles, and social context that shape our legal

system.

It is a notable historical reality that despite

two hundred and thirty-six years passing since the

ratification of the Constitution, Congress has yet to

amend the constitution to introduce accountability

and transparency measures to the Supreme Court of

the United States. This absence of amendments has

allowed the nomination and confirmation process

for Supreme Court justices to become increasingly

politicized, deviating from the desired standards.

Presidents often nominate candidates who align

with their own ideological leanings, using the court

as a means to further their own agendas.

Consequently, the confirmation process in the

Senate has transformed into intense partisan battles,

worsening the problem.

The intense partisanship surrounding the

confirmation process has the potential to

compromise the court's independence and

neutrality. Justices may find themselves influenced

by political considerations rather than strictly

adhering to a diligent interpretation of the law. This

politicization undermines the court's role as an

impartial arbiter and weakens public trust in its

decisions.

Remarkably, despite this persistent issue, Congress has not taken steps to address the matter through constitutional amendments, leaving the process susceptible to ongoing political influence. The absence of accountability and transparency measures within the Supreme Court's nomination and confirmation procedures continues to be a subject of concern. The Supreme Court's lack of diversity, both in terms of professional background and demographic representation, has been a point of criticism. Some argue that a more diverse court would better reflect the interests and experiences of the American people and promote a broader range of perspectives in the decision-making process.

\#

Recent events involving justices of the Supreme Court have raised significant concerns about their ethical and moral conduct, highlighting actions that deviate from widely accepted principles, values, and standards of right and wrong. While the constitutionality of the Supreme Court is accepted, it is crucial to address and criticize instances of corruption that have appeared within its ranks.

The Supreme Court, regarded as the ultimate arbiter of the Constitution, holds a well-established position within the U.S. governmental system.

Altering the court's structure or operations needs

constitutional amendments or legislative measures.

However, despite the United States' founding as a

Federalist Republic rather than a monarchy on the

other hand, the Supreme Court law of the land has

evolved into a perilous monarchy, featuring

invulnerable members appointed for life.

#

The United States Congress, afflicted by

inadequate self-governance and a substantial

disconnection from reality, allows Supreme Court

members to partake in misconduct without meeting

any repercussions. This worrisome scenario has led

to grave political consequences, as the political philosophies of constituents, regardless of party affiliation, vary across different regions of the United States. Thus, the Supreme Court continues to run independently, governed by its own set of rules, while evading accountability for their actions.

A justice of the Supreme Court can be removed from office through the process of impeachment. The Constitution grants the power of impeachment to the House of Representatives, which can start the proceedings by bringing forth formal charges, also known as articles of impeachment. Impeachment can be based on various grounds, including treason, bribery, or other high crimes and misdemeanors.

The Supreme Court's track record exposes its ineffectiveness, revealing a disturbing pattern of regressive decisions that have had significant repercussions for minorities, women, civil liberties, and the right to abortion, just to mention a few. Far from upholding justice, the Court has perpetuated systemic inequalities and undermined fundamental rights, calling into question its ability to fulfill its role as a fair and impartial arbiter.

#

Throughout history, the Supreme Court has played a pivotal role in addressing issues of racial segregation and discrimination. However, its decisions have often fallen short of delivering true justice for minority communities. From the infamous Plessy v. Ferguson ruling, which upheld "separate but equal" segregation, to recent decisions that have weakened voting rights protections, the Court has at times enabled rather than dismantled discriminatory practices, perpetuating inequality, and marginalization.

Similarly, the Supreme Court's treatment of women's rights has been a cause for concern. While landmark decisions like Roe v. Wade recognized a woman's right to choose, subsequent rulings have chipped away at reproductive rights, imposing burdensome restrictions and eroding access to safe and legal abortion, plus the reversal of Roe v Wade in 2022. These decisions have disproportionately affected marginalized women, who face more barriers to healthcare and reproductive autonomy.

Moreover, the Court has shown a tendency to prioritize perceived national security interests over civil liberties. From endorsing warrantless surveillance in the name of counterterrorism to upholding policies that target specific religious or ethnic groups, the Court has eroded the very

principles that protect individual rights and

freedoms.

The ineffectiveness of the Supreme Court in

safeguarding marginalized communities, women's

rights, civil liberties, and the right to abortion is a

cause for deep concern. Its decisions have

perpetuated systemic injustices, leaving these

communities vulnerable to ongoing discrimination

and infringement upon their basic rights.

It is crucial for the Court to recommit itself to

the principles of justice and equality. This requires

justices who are willing to interpret the law with a

broader perspective, considering the historical context and the impact of their decisions on marginalized populations. Additionally, advocacy efforts and public pressure must continue to push for reforms that prioritize the protection of civil liberties, equal rights, and reproductive autonomy.

Again, it is imperative for the Supreme Court to rise above its ineffectiveness and fulfill its duty to uphold justice for all, regardless of race, gender, or socioeconomic status. Only through a renewed commitment to fairness and equality can the Court regain its credibility and ensure the protection of fundamental rights for all individuals in our society.

#

One aspect is the influence of non-living entities, such as corporations, in electoral processes. The Supreme Court's Citizens United decision in 2010 allowed corporations and unions to spend unlimited amounts of money in support of political candidates. This ruling has raised concerns about the potential distortion of democratic processes and the disproportionate influence of wealth and corporate interests in elections. Critics argue that this increased influence can hinder the representation of marginalized groups, including women and minorities, who may face additional barriers to taking part and influencing the political landscape. Women and minorities have historically faced systemic obstacles and discrimination in electoral processes. Voter suppression efforts, gerrymandering, and restrictive voter identification laws disproportionately affect these communities, making it more challenging for them to exercise their right to vote and have their voices heard.

The Supreme Court's potential conflict of interest on non-living entities, women, minorities, and marginalized communities in the context of elections is a matter of concern and debate.

A specific angle to consider is the matter of campaign finance and the influential impact of inanimate entities, such as corporations, on elections. The Court's rulings, particularly Citizens United v. FEC, have expanded the ability of these entities to contribute financially to political campaigns, leading to concerns about the disproportionate impact of moneyed interests on elections. This can marginalize the voices of women, minorities, and other marginalized communities, as they may lack the financial resources and access to contribute at the same level as these non-living entities.

Furthermore, the potential conflict arises from the composition of the Court itself. Justices are appointed by the President and confirmed by the Senate, leading to a political appointment process. This political nature of the appointments can create the belief of bias or conflicts of interest in cases related to elections and marginalized communities. Concerns are raised when justices may have affiliations, biases, or connections to entities or interests that could influence their decisions on matters affecting the entire population but with a more severe impact on women, minorities, and marginalized communities.

The Court's decisions on voting rights and election-related laws can also affect women, minorities, and marginalized communities. Cases related to voter ID requirements, gerrymandering, and the Voting Rights Act have generated significant debates about the potential for disenfranchisement and the dilution of minority voting power. It is arguable that certain rulings have weakened voting rights protections, making it more challenging for these communities to take part in the electoral process and have their voices heard.

It is crucial to ensure that the Court keeps its independence, impartiality, and commitment to upholding the rights and equal representation of all individuals, irrespective of their backgrounds or the influence of non-living entities.

#

The recognition of constitutional rights for non-living entities by the Supreme Court, while denying certain constitutional rights primarily to women, has ignited passionate debates and raised profound concerns about the equilibrium of legal protections in our society. This clear inconsistency serves as a stark reminder of the intricate nature of constitutional interpretation and the ever-evolving landscape of our legal system.

The acknowledgment of constitutional rights for non-living entities, including corporations, originates from the understanding that certain rights, such as freedom of speech and religious expression, extend to entities composed of individuals. However, in the realm of women's reproductive rights, the court has taken a different stance, often deferring to states' interests in regulating abortion. This divergence exposes a systemic devaluation of women's autonomy and bodily integrity, which curtails their ability to make decisions about their reproductive health.

There is no justifiable reason why women should not be granted the same level of constitutional protection as other entities, and why their fundamental right to choose should not be upheld. It is crucial to recognize that women's rights advocates argue that such limitations disproportionately affect marginalized communities and impede access to essential healthcare. They call for a more comprehensive understanding of reproductive rights, one that takes into consideration the physical, emotional, and socioeconomic well-being of women.

As the legal landscape continues to evolve, with limited progress on women's issues, it becomes imperative for society to engage in thoughtful discussions concerning the interpretation and application of constitutional rights. It is only through these conversations that we can ensure equal protection for all individuals, irrespective of their gender.

#

The lifetime tenure of Supreme Court Justices, as outlined in the U.S. Constitution, serves as a fascinating aspect that aims to safeguard the judiciary's independence. Nevertheless, this provision has sparked ongoing debates regarding its impact on the Court's long-term dynamics and its implications for modern governance. On one hand, proponents argue that lifetime appointments offer stability and shield the judiciary from political interference. However, critics contend that this system can lead to situations where Justices serve for extended periods, potentially ignoring their performance or disregarding evolving societal values.

The Framers of the Constitution introduced lifetime appointments with the intention of establishing an independent and separate judiciary capable of upholding the rule of law and interpreting the Constitution without undue influence from other branches of government. Despite this noble aim, the Supreme Court's actual performance has not always aligned perfectly with these principles.

Instead of repeatedly complaining to the same individuals about the same issues, and expecting a different result, it is time to break free from this cycle of insanity. We should advocate for a constitutional amendment on the appointment of

new Supreme Court Justices. This amendment

would stipulate that any future Justice appointment

must secure a supermajority vote in both the House

and the Senate. By demanding this change, we can

work towards a more balanced and consensus-

based approach to Supreme Court appointments.

The proposal to amend the Constitution and

require a supermajority approval in both the Senate

and the House for Supreme Court Justices'

appointments presents itself as a compelling and

fitting solution to address the prevailing and

escalating societal discontent with the Court's

functioning. This approach seeks to tackle the issues of political polarization and partisan influence that have plagued the nomination and confirmation process of Justices for years.

By demanding a supermajority vote, this amendment aims to introduce a higher threshold for consensus, encouraging elected officials to collaborate across party lines and consider candidates with broader appeal and support. It recognizes the need to transcend the entrenched divisions that have sometimes characterized Supreme Court nominations, leading to contentious and highly politicized confirmations.

Moreover, this solution resonates with the concerns of a society looking for a more balanced and accountable judiciary. The supermajority requirement instills a sense of responsibility and deliberation among elected officials, urging them to choose candidates who embody impartiality, integrity, and expertise. It shifts the focus away from partisan interests and political maneuvering, aligning the process with the fundamental principles of fairness and justice.

The growing public discontent with the current state of the Supreme Court process needs a reform that promotes greater transparency and public confidence. By endorsing a supermajority vote, elected officials can prove a commitment to ensuring that future Justices enjoy broader support and reflect the diverse perspectives of the American populace.

However, as with any constitutional amendment, this proposal will likely meet rigorous debate and face challenges in the legislative process. Elected officials with differing ideological perspectives will need to come together to build a bipartisan consensus around the amendment's merits and implications. It will require a collective effort to overcome any potential resistance and safeguard the integrity of the amendment's

purpose.

In conclusion, the call for amending the

Constitution to mandate a supermajority vote in

both the Senate and the House for Supreme Court

Justices' appointments reflects a pragmatic and

suitable response to the growing concerns

surrounding the Court's functionality. This solution,

while catering to the sensibilities of elected officials,

also holds the potential to restore public faith in the

Court's independence and ensure that future

appointments stand on a solid foundation of

bipartisan support and judicial competence.

The time has come for our elected representatives in the House and the Senate to step up and act by amending the Constitution to require a supermajority vote for appointing Supreme Court Justices. It's essential for our democracy to evolve and address the challenges we face today, particularly the increasing polarization and gridlock that have infiltrated our judicial nomination process.

As our nation grows and becomes more diverse, the stakes surrounding Supreme Court appointments are higher than ever. The decisions made by these Justices can shape the trajectory of our society for generations. Yet, in recent times, we have seen contentious and divisive confirmation battles, where partisan interests seem to outweigh the importance of selecting qualified and impartial candidates.

By demanding a supermajority vote, we demand a higher standard of agreement and collaboration. It is time for our elected officials to prioritize the welfare of the nation over their political ambitions. A supermajority requirement compels them to come together, transcending party lines, to find common ground and name candidates who have demonstrated exceptional legal expertise, ethical conduct, and a commitment to upholding the Constitution.

This move is not about stifling diversity of opinion or limiting the importance of varying perspectives. Instead, it is about ensuring that appointments to the Supreme Court reflect the broader will of the American people and garner support beyond a narrow ideological spectrum. It is about fostering a judiciary that inspires trust, confidence, and respect among citizens from all walks of life.

Some may argue that amending the Constitution in this manner could be a challenging and time-consuming process, and they would be

right. However, the difficulty should not deter us

from pursuing meaningful change. The journey to a

supermajority requirement for Justices'

appointments might be arduous, but it is a journey

worth undertaking for the sake of our democracy's

future.

Furthermore, such an amendment would

send a powerful message to the nation that our

elected representatives are willing to set aside

partisan bickering and prioritize the interests of the

American people. It will showcase their willingness

to put on their "big boys' pants" and address the issues that genuinely matter to the public.

We are at a critical juncture where the credibility and integrity of our institutions hang in the balance. It is time for the House and the Senate to rise to the occasion, show leadership, and prove their commitment to a fair and balanced judiciary. Amending the Constitution to require a supermajority vote for Supreme Court appointments is not just an act of political courage; it is a duty to protect and strengthen the very foundations of our democracy.

The call for the House and the Senate to "put on big boys' pants" and amend the Constitution for a supermajority requirement in appointing Supreme Court Justices is a rallying cry for a more inclusive and responsible democracy. It challenges our elected officials to rise above partisan squabbles, prioritize the nation's well-being, and restore the faith of the American people in the institutions that govern us all.

Further into this matter, a span of twenty-four years within the realm of US politics translates to the duration of six presidential terms, essentially being a single generation. It is proposed that there should be limitations imposed on the tenures of Supreme Court justices. This idea aligns with the concept that Congress has the authority to enact legislation instituting term boundaries for these justices. Notably, the Constitution does not explicitly define a specific length for the terms of Supreme Court justices, thereby granting Congress the jurisdiction to set up such constraints through statutory means. However, to execute this arrangement, a constitutional amendment would be necessary to prevent potential conflicts with the principle of separation of powers and the autonomy of the judicial system.

Regrettably, the Congressional body in Washington tends to be where promising concepts falter and fade, as the institution's track record is lacking in noteworthy contributions, achievements, and acknowledgment from the broader populace. In the present day, the most significant threat to America comes from internal factors rather than external ones, with the inertia of Congress being a particularly noteworthy concern.

www.ingramcontent.com/pod-product-compliance
Lightning Source LLC
Chambersburg PA
CBHW050811260726

48660CB00004B/1360